CH

WORLD LEADERS

KIM JONG UN

SUPREME LEADER OF NORTH KOREA

by Russell Roberts

FOCUS READERS

FOCUS READERS

www.focusreaders.com

Focus Readers is distributed by North Star Editions:
sales@northstareditions.com | 888-417-0195

Produced for Focus Readers by Red Line Editorial.

Content Consultant: James Matray, Professor of History, California State University, Chico

Photographs ©: Wong Maye-E/AP Images, cover, 1; narvikk/iStockphoto, 4–5, 12; Kyodo/AP Images, 7; Anton_Ivanov/Shutterstock Images, 8–9; Red Line Editorial, 11, 36; Bulgac/iStockphoto, 15; Korea News Service/AP Images, 16–17; David Guttenfelder/AP Images, 19; Goddard_Photography/iStockphoto, 21, 31; KRT/APTN/AP Images, 22–23; Peter Schneider/Keystone/AP Images, 25; Kim Kwang Hyon/AP Images, 27; Kyodo/Newscom, 28–29; Korean Central News Agency/Korea News Service/AP Images, 32; KCNA/Reuters/Newscom, 34–35; Matej Hudovernik/iStockphoto, 39; Mark Schiefelbein/AP Images, 41; Gao Haorong/Xinhua/AP Images, 42–43; Ahn Young-joon/AP Images, 44

ISBN
978-1-63517-547-9 (hardcover)
978-1-63517-619-3 (paperback)
978-1-63517-763-3 (ebook pdf)
978-1-63517-691-9 (hosted ebook)

Library of Congress Control Number: 2017948130

Printed in the United States of America
Mankato, MN
November, 2017

ABOUT THE AUTHOR

Russell Roberts is an award-winning writer who has written more than 75 books for children and adults. Included among his books for adults are *Down the Jersey Shore* and *Rediscover the Hidden New Jersey*. Among his children's books are biographies, examinations of famous buildings, and stories about characters from Greek mythology.

TABLE OF CONTENTS

CHAPTER 1

REMOVED!

On December 8, 2013, a large meeting took place in North Korea's capital city of Pyongyang. The meeting included many government officials. Among them was Kim Jong Un, the Supreme Leader of North Korea.

Jang Song Thaek also attended. He was the vice chairman of the National Defense Commission. Many experts considered Jang the second-most powerful person in the country.

Pyongyang is North Korea's most advanced city. Citizens need permission to live there.

Jang had been advising Kim since December 2011, when Kim first took office.

Two police officers interrupted the meeting to confront Jang. As everyone watched, the officers arrested and removed Jang from the building.

After he was arrested, the government-run Korean Central News Agency (KCNA) made a broadcast. The broadcast accused Jang of criminal acts. It accused Jang of being corrupt, taking drugs, and other crimes. KCNA blamed Jang for poor management of North Korea's finances. The news agency said Jang only pretended to be loyal to Kim.

Days later, Jang's jailers brought him to a North Korean military academy. There he was forced to watch the execution of two of his top assistants. The executions were so brutal that Jang fainted. Days later, he was killed in the same way.

Jang Song Thaek and Kim Jong Un appeared at a military parade together in 2012.

Kim had watched the officers arrest Jang. Foreign government experts suspected that Kim had ordered the arrests and executions. Since becoming North Korea's leader, Kim had **purged** numerous people. He feared that they might plot against him. So in some respects, what happened to Jang was not surprising. What was surprising, however, was that Kim had done this to his uncle.

CHAPTER 2

THE GREAT LEADER

Kim Jong Un is the third member of his family to lead North Korea. The other two were his grandfather Kim Il Sung and father Kim Jong Il.

Kim Il Sung was born in 1912. As a young man, he became a **Communist**. He fought the Japanese, who had ruled Korea since 1910. In late 1940, Kim went to the Soviet Union and lived in a military camp. He spent the remainder of World War II (1939–1945) in the Soviet Union.

The Juche Tower contains 25,550 blocks, marking the number of days in Kim Il Sung's life.

The war ended with Japan's surrender in 1945. Afterward, the United States and the Soviet Union divided Korea into two military zones. The Soviet Union occupied the northern half, and the United States occupied the southern half. The Soviet Union was a Communist country. Its leaders wanted a Communist government in North Korea.

In September 1945, the Soviets brought Kim Il Sung back to North Korea. They hoped to establish him as a future leader. Kim soon became chairman of a Communist group called the Provisional People's Committee. To help Kim gain power, the Soviet military police arrested the Communists' political opponents.

From 1945 to 1948, the North Korean government operated under the control of the Soviet Union. On September 9, 1948, the North formally became the Democratic People's

Republic of Korea (DPRK). Kim Il Sung was named premier, making him the most important government official. Less than a month earlier, the South officially became the Republic of Korea (ROK). Its capital city was Seoul.

NORTH KOREA'S BORDERS

CHINA

NORTH KOREA

★ National capital
····· International border
····· Demilitarized Zone

★ Pyongyang

SEA OF JAPAN

★ Seoul

YELLOW SEA

SOUTH KOREA

N
W ✦ E
S

▲ The Mansu Grand Monument in North Korea features a statue of Kim Il Sung.

Kim Il Sung wanted to unify North and South Korea. He thought a war with South Korea would be quick. In June 1950, Kim's army invaded the South, beginning the Korean War. But the war lasted longer than planned. More than one million North Koreans died. Finally, in July 1953, the two sides signed an **armistice**. This agreement established the modern border between North and South Korea.

In 1955, Kim Il Sung introduced North Korea to his concept of Juche (*Joo*-cheh), or self-reliance. Juche encourages North Koreans to rely on themselves instead of outsiders. According to Kim, self-reliance could only be achieved through obedience to a great leader. This concept helped Kim maintain power.

Kim Il Sung held office for more than 45 years. He was known as the Suryong, or Great Leader. After his death in 1994, his body was preserved. It lies in a large building where citizens go to see it.

THINK ABOUT IT ◁

What other countries can you think of that are or have been divided?

FOCUS ON
NORTH KOREA

North Korea occupies the northern part of the Korean Peninsula. People first came to the Korean Peninsula around 6000 BCE. Today, approximately 25 million people live in North Korea. Its capital, Pyongyang, is located in the west-central region of the nation.

North Korea has a Communist government, led by a supreme leader. The country's official religion is **atheism**. However, the country's most practiced religions are Buddhism and Confucianism. The nation's official language is Korean.

The area that separates North and South Korea is called the Demilitarized Zone. It is 148 miles (238 km) long and 2.5 miles (4.0 km) wide. It is the most battle-ready area in the world. But it also serves as an unofficial wildlife preserve.

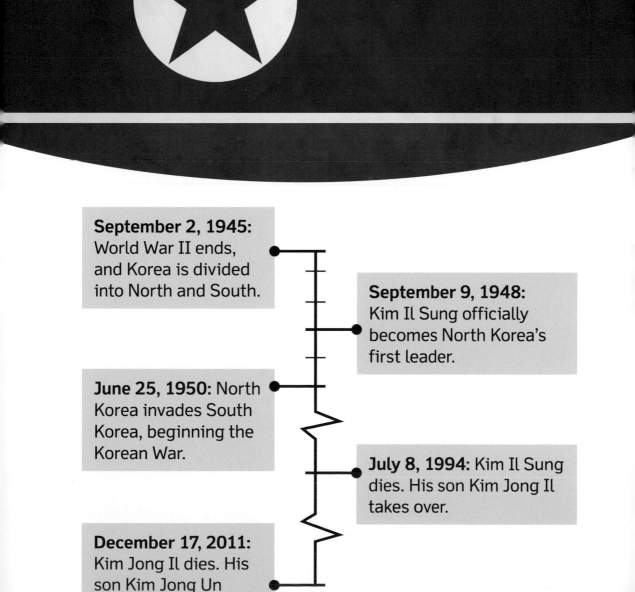

September 2, 1945: World War II ends, and Korea is divided into North and South.

September 9, 1948: Kim Il Sung officially becomes North Korea's first leader.

June 25, 1950: North Korea invades South Korea, beginning the Korean War.

July 8, 1994: Kim Il Sung dies. His son Kim Jong Il takes over.

December 17, 2011: Kim Jong Il dies. His son Kim Jong Un takes over.

CHAPTER 3

LIKE FATHER, LIKE SON

Kim Il Sung's son Kim Jong Il **succeeded** him as the leader of North Korea in 1994. His official slogan was "expect no change from me." As with Kim Il Sung, the North Korean people showed great respect to Kim Jong Il. They called him the Dear Leader.

Like today, North Koreans were required to admire the Kims. Portraits of Kim Il Sung and Kim Jong Il hung in every office, classroom, and home.

Kim Jong Il waves to a crowd after more than a year in office.

In school, all music, storybooks, and artwork were about the leaders. At seven years old, kids joined the Children's Union. This group taught children to worship the Kims.

Similar to his father, Kim Jong Il placed many restrictions on North Korean society. Even today, North Korea remains a very restrictive nation. Many North Koreans have no access to the internet. Citizens need a permit to travel anywhere in the country.

To enforce its rules, the government keeps close watch of its people. Neighborhood units monitor people's personal activities. If citizens fail to obey government rules, they can be sent to prison camps. By one estimate, approximately one million people have died in the camps.

Kim Jong Il faced challenges that were passed on from his father's time in power. For years, the

Soviet Union had provided foreign aid to North

Korea. But in 1987, the Soviet Union's economy

weakened, and the nation stopped this aid. The

Soviet Union and China also started making

North Korea pay money for imported goods.

Previously, North Korea had obtained these goods by **barter**.

North Korea could not buy as many imports as it had obtained by barter. As a result, the country received less petroleum and fertilizer. There was not enough fuel for farmers' tractors or fertilizer to help crops grow.

To make things worse, massive rainstorms hit in 1995. The next year, there was a drought. The change in weather and lack of fuel caused a severe **famine** from 1994 to 1998. As many as 2.45 million people may have died from starvation. One report states that, in some areas, 85 percent of children did not have enough food.

News of the famine was slow to emerge. Other countries often know little about what's happening inside North Korea. Outsiders have called the nation the Hermit Kingdom for years.

▲ Portraits of the first two North Korean leaders hang in Kim Il Sung Square in Pyongyang.

However, when the news of the famine finally got out, many nations sent food.

When Kim Jong Il died on December 17, 2011, North Korea still was not producing enough food for its people. This was only one problem that Kim Jong Un faced when he succeeded his father as North Korea's new leader.

CHAPTER 4

YOUNG KIM

The secretive nature of North Korea makes information about Kim Jong Un difficult to find. Even his birth date is uncertain. Historians agree on the day of January 8, but they debate his birth year. South Korean intelligence services and the US Treasury Department both report that Kim was born in 1984. However, Kim himself claims he was born in 1983.

Kim Jong Un attended his father's funeral in December 2011.

Kim Jong Un is the third and youngest son of Kim Jong Il. Kim Jong Un's mother, Ko Young Hee, was an opera singer, as well as Kim Jong Il's second wife. She supposedly pushed for Kim Jong Un to be his father's successor.

Kim Jong Un had a brother, Kim Jong Chol, and a half brother, Kim Jong Nam. Of the three, Kim Jong Un was reportedly his father's favorite. Kim Jong Il believed they shared similar personality traits. Kim Jong Un's half sister, Kim Sul Song, and sister, Kim Yo Jong, were also favorites with their father.

In the late 1990s, young Kim Jong Un went to school in Switzerland. He attended the International School of Berne and the Liebefeld Steinhölzli. At Liebefeld Steinhölzli, Kim's true identity was a secret. On the first day of school, he wore jeans, a Chicago Bulls sweatshirt, and

▲ Liebefeld Steinhölzli is near the Swiss capital of Bern, where foreign diplomats are often stationed.

Nike athletic shoes. He seemed like an average student. His classmates and teachers knew him as a skinny boy named Un Pak. They thought his father was a North Korean **diplomat**.

Kim's classmates remember him as a quiet homebody. Nevertheless, he was fairly popular.

His classmates recall his keen sense of humor, his great collection of Nikes, and talking with him about soccer. They say he got along with everyone, including people from countries that were not friendly with North Korea.

According to his classmates, Kim loved the Chicago Bulls. His favorite player was Michael Jordan. Kim loved playing basketball, too. He was a playmaker on the court—the one who made things happen. He loved to win and hated to lose.

In addition to basketball, Kim participated in soccer and skiing. He also enjoyed playing video games. In school, Kim had average grades. He struggled with classes taught in German and English. However, his grades did not bother him.

Kim's schooling in Switzerland ended in 2000. Upon his return to North Korea, Kim attended Kim Il Sung Military University in Pyongyang.

▲ Former Chicago Bulls player Dennis Rodman visited
North Korea in 2014 to celebrate Kim's birthday.

Kim's brother Kim Jong Chol may have gone to the
military school at the same time. Initially, experts
on North Korea did not consider Kim Jong Un
to be a contender to succeed his father. Foreign
analysts focused on his siblings instead.

CHAPTER 5

NEXT IN LINE

In May 2001, Kim Jong Un's brother Kim Jong Nam was arrested in Japan. He had been trying to go to Disneyland with a fake passport. The embarrassing incident caused Kim Jong Nam to fall out of favor with his father.

Kim Jong Il did not think his middle son, Kim Jong Chol, was fit for the job, either. According to some sources, Kim Jong Il thought his son was "unmanly." Both brothers were out of the running.

Kim Jong Nam's fake passport had the name Pang Xiong, or "Fat Bear."

As a result, Kim Jong Un moved to the top of the list for succession.

Around 2007, Kim Jong Un started joining his father to inspect weapons and soldiers. He also began receiving important political and military titles. For instance, he became a four-star general, as well as deputy chairman of the Central Military Commission of the Workers' Party. He also joined the Central Committee. This was a small group of Communist party members with great political power.

In 2009, Kim started gaining weight. Analysts suspected he was trying to look more like his grandfather, Kim Il Sung. A Korean belief, *gyeok se yu jeon,* stated that boys were more like their grandfather than their father. If Kim Jong Un looked like his grandfather, he could possibly gain greater favor with the public. Many North Koreans

▲ The North Korean government often uses media, such as posters, to gain public support.

wanted to know that Kim Il Sung was still with them. They hoped the leader would lead them through his grandson.

The North Korean government continued to paint Kim Jong Un in a good light. The media portrayed him as a military genius. According to the media, Kim could drive tanks, operate complex weapons systems, and pilot helicopters.

⚜ In 2010, Kim Jong Un (left) celebrated the 65th birthday of the Workers' Party of Korea with his father (right).

He also began appearing in North Korean stories and poems written about his father.

By late 2011, a subtle change occurred in Kim Jong Un's media presence. Previously, Kim had been grouped with his father's assistants during television appearances. But now, he appeared at his father's side. It was obvious to viewers that young Kim was an important person like his father. When Kim Jong Il died, North Koreans would expect Kim Jong Un to take over.

Kim Jong Un was approximately 27 years old when he became the Supreme Leader of North Korea in 2011. He was the world's youngest head of state. North Koreans, however, did not view Kim's youthfulness as a positive trait. They wanted their leader to have years of wisdom. As it turned out, wisdom was exactly what Kim needed to handle North Korea's many challenges.

THINK ABOUT IT ◁

What are some advantages and disadvantages of having a young leader?

CHAPTER 6

SUPREME LEADER

Kim Jong Un made his first public appearance as Supreme Leader on April 15, 2012. It was the 100th anniversary of the birthday of his grandfather, Kim Il Sung.

Only a few months later, the country announced that Kim Jong Un had a wife, Ri Sol Ju. Ri had short hair and wore American- and European-style clothes. Some analysts suggest that Ri helped Kim display a friendly public image.

Kim and his wife attended an amusement park opening in 2012.

The couple has been shown visiting an amusement park and attending a concert with Disney characters. While out, Kim would take pictures with admirers.

Behind the scenes, Kim had his work cut out for him. One item on his agenda was economic

NORTH KOREAN ECONOMIC ZONES

CHINA

Pyongyang

SOUTH KOREA

Ec Economic development
A Agricultural development
I Industrial development
Ex Export processing
T Tourism development
H High-tech development

reform. In 2013, he adopted the Farmland Responsibility System. This reform encouraged farmers to grow more food by allowing them to keep a portion of their crops. Prior to this policy, farmers had to give all their crops to the government.

As a result of the reform, North Korea had a record harvest in 2013. A larger harvest meant that North Korea could purchase less food from other countries. This saved the government money. With more crops to export, North Korea took in more money, too.

Another of Kim's reforms allowed workers to earn more money the harder they worked. Kim established special zones where workers competed against one another. The hardest workers received the highest pay. In turn, they could buy high-ticket items, such as new cars.

Previously, people could only get expensive goods by showing loyalty to the government.

Greater wealth for North Koreans brought other changes, too. Today, more people in the country use cell phones, drive cars, and wear colorful clothes. North Korea even has a tourist destination called the Masik Pass Ski Resort.

In some ways, Kim's changes seem to be working. But in other ways, North Korea remains a dangerous place. One example is Kim's purging of government officials. To avoid losing power, Kim sends people he views as threats either to prison or to be killed. The purged officials disappear from public view.

Not even Kim's family members are safe from purges. First, he removed his uncle Jang Song Thaek. Then, in February 2017, Kim's half brother Kim Jong Nam was murdered at an airport in

▲ Kim has added color to many capital buildings in an attempt to attract tourists.

Malaysia. He was likely killed by North Korean agents. They used a deadly chemical weapon called VX. Analysts think Kim Jong Un might have felt threatened by his half brother.

Kim Jong Un's dangerous actions have drawn the concern of countries around the world. Above all, countries fear Kim's missile testing. Analysts, political leaders, and global citizens fear the tests could erupt into war.

FOCUS ON
XI JINPING

Similar to North Korea, the People's Republic of China is a Communist country. The nation has been one of North Korea's closest allies. In 2013, Xi Jinping became the president of China.

Xi was likely born in 1953. His father was a companion of Mao Zedong, the legendary Chinese Communist leader. In 1974, Xi joined the Chinese Communist Party (CCP). In the following years, Xi held a series of jobs in the CCP. In 2008, Xi was elected vice president of China.

China's size and power in the world make the nation a useful ally to North Korea. During the Korean War, China provided North Korea with support. But in recent years, the relationship between the two countries has weakened.

While Kim Jong Il visited China often, Kim Jong Un and Xi are not in close contact. Some analysts

 Xi Jinping and Kim Jong Un are approximately 30 years apart in age.

think the leaders' lack of relationship stems from their large age difference. Compared to Xi, Kim Jong Un is young and inexperienced.

Kim's weapons testing is a major source of tension between the two leaders. While not a target of the weapons, China is dangerously close to Kim's testing areas. The country would be placed in even more danger if Kim's activity resulted in war.

CHAPTER 7

AN UNCERTAIN FUTURE

In January 2016, North Korea claimed it had tested its first hydrogen bomb. The claim raised worldwide concern. North Korea had tested its first **nuclear** weapon in 2006. Nations worried about the growing power of these weapons.

Since taking power, Kim Jong Un has repeatedly tested dangerous weapons. North Korea has tested more missiles under his leadership than under Kim Il Sung and Kim Jong Il combined.

North Korea destroyed a weapons facility in 2008 as part of a promise to stop making bombs.

North Korean defectors and South Koreans protest against the North Korean government.

In response to Kim's tests, the United Nations imposed **sanctions** on North Korea. These sanctions made goods scarcer and more expensive. North Koreans had experienced sanctions in the past. But according to some citizens, this time the effect was more severe.

Kim's weapons testing has also increased tensions between North Korea and the United States. US leaders worry that Kim is trying to develop a missile to attack the United States. However, Kim insists North Korea has the right to develop weapons against a US attack. Each side is suspicious of the other. In September 2017, North Korea conducted a major nuclear test. US leaders responded that any threats from North Korea would be met with military action. Many observers fear the tension could result in war.

Between the possibility of war and a struggling economy, Kim Jong Un faces many challenges. Not all North Koreans are loyal. Some try to escape the country by **defecting**. Still, decades of loyalty to the Kim family has kept the leader's power intact. And with secrecy on Kim's side, world leaders are unsure of what Kim will do next.

THINK ABOUT IT ◄

How would you behave toward North Korea if you were the president of the United States?

FOCUS ON
KIM JONG UN

Write your answers on a separate piece of paper.

1. Write a summary of how Kim Jong Un came to power.

2. What decisions would you make if you were the leader of North Korea? Why?

3. What is the correct order of North Korea's three Supreme Leaders, beginning with the first?

    A. Kim Jong Un, Kim Il Sung, Kim Jong Il

    B. Kim Jong Il, Kim Jong Un, Kim Il Sung

    C. Kim Il Sung, Kim Jong Il, Kim Jong Un

4. Why did the United Nations place sanctions on North Korea?

    A. to free up resources for South Korea

    B. to force Kim to stop testing missiles

    C. to punish the North Korean people

Answer key on page 48.

GLOSSARY

armistice
An agreement to temporarily stop fighting.

atheism
The belief that there is no god.

barter
To trade goods for other goods, instead of paying with money.

Communist
Someone who belongs to a political party that believes the government should own all property.

defecting
Leaving a cause or a country for another.

diplomat
A person who represents his or her country's government.

famine
An extreme shortage of food.

nuclear
Relating to atomic bombs.

purged
Removed, often leading to execution.

reform
Changes put in place to improve or fix problems.

sanctions
Penalties intended to force a desired effect.

succeeded
Replaced a previous leader.

TO LEARN MORE

BOOKS

O'Neal, Claire. *We Visit North Korea*. Hockessin, DE: Mitchell Lane Publishers, 2014.

Senker, Cath. *North Korea and South Korea*. New York: Rosen Publishing, 2013.

Sonneborn, Liz. *North Korea*. New York: Children's Press, 2014.

NOTE TO EDUCATORS

Visit **www.focusreaders.com** to find lesson plans, activities, links, and other resources related to this title.

INDEX

Answer Key: 1. Answers will vary; **2.** Answers will vary; **3.** C; **4.** B